5

of the

AMERICAN
REPUBLIC

*The Founding Principles
That Made America Great*

The First Continental Congress at Prayer

Eddie L. Hyatt

HYATT PRESS * 2018

5 PILLARS OF THE AMERICAN REPUBLIC

By Eddie L. Hyatt

Published by Hyatt Press
A Subsidiary of Hyatt Int'l Ministries, Incorporated

Mailing Address (2018)
Hyatt Int'l Ministries
P.O. Box 3877
Grapevine, TX 76099-3877

Internet Addresses
Email: dreddiehyatt@gmail.com
Web Site: www.eddiehyatt.com
Social Media: Eddie L. Hyatt

Unless otherwise indicated, all Scripture quotations are taken from the New Kings James Version of the Bible. © 1979, 1980, 1982 by Thomas Nelson, Inc. Publishers.

ISBN: 978-1-888435-59-7

Printed in the United States of America

"Unless the people of this nation take seriously the storm flags waving, we are doomed to repeat the past mistakes of those who refused to pay attention to history and end up in the graveyard of fallen nations."

Ronald M. Mann, Deputy Director
Commission on the Bicentennial
of the United States Constitution

Table of Contents

Preface

This book is written out of a passionate desire to see America rediscover her Christian roots and live out the noble vision of her Founders. They envisioned a nation of godly, moral people who would enjoy the fruit of their own labor in true liberty and freedom.

I had given hope of America ever recapturing this vision, but in 2010 my hope was renewed by an unexpected encounter with the Lord. I received hope that we "could" see another Great Spiritual Awakening that would revive and renew the churches of America, impact our culture and stem the tide of immorality, secularism and false religion that is destroying our land.

A necessary key for seeing this happen is recovering the founding principles—those pillars--on which this nation was built. This is vital, for as George Orwell said in his classic book, *1984*, "Whoever controls the past, controls the future."

This small book is sent forth with the prayer that it will be used far and wide to awaken this generation to this nation's true origins and thereby ignite faith for its present and its future.

Chapter I

Introduction

America was founded on Christian principles and values. It was not founded as a theocracy. Theocratic rulers claim a Divine right to rule over their subjects. America's founders held no such grandiose view of themselves or any human being, and they had rejected the theocratic claims of popes, priests, and monarchs. They had not, however, rejected Christianity.

America's Founders, for the most part, identified with the mindset of those they called "dissenting Protestants." The dissenting Protestant insisted that civil government should have no role in the church nor in matters of faith and conscience. Freedom from government tyranny in matters of faith was an ideal that pervaded the thinking of America's Founders.

However, for there to be liberty without license, the Founders knew that the populace would have to be governed from within by virtuous values. That is why they all agreed that only Christianity provided the moral values and intellectual underpinnings for a stable and prosperous nation.

The Founders were flawed human beings, but they were people of integrity committed to a set of values based on the teachings of Jesus and the New Testament. Despite their human shortcomings, they did a remarkable job of bringing forth a new kind of nation, in the words of Abraham Lincoln, "conceived in liberty and dedicated to the proposition that all men [people] are created equal."

Here are the 5 pillars on which the American Republic was founded.

Chapter 2

Pillar I
Belief in God as the Creator
and Moral Governor of the Universe

The Founders considered belief in the God of the Bible as being essential for good citizenship. Unless the citizens would have a moral sense of obligation to their Creator, they would tend to live selfish, unrestrained lives, harmful to society.

This was expressed by James Madison when he wrote, "Before any man can be considered as a member of civil society, he must be considered as a subject of the Governor of the Universe." Madison also wrote,

> The belief in a God All Powerful wise and good, is so essential to the moral order of the world and to the happiness of man, that arguments which enforce it cannot be drawn from too many sources nor adapted with too much solicitude to the different characters and capacities impressed with it (Hyatt, *Pilgrims and Patriots*, 131).

The Founders functioned on the assumption of a Divine Creator to whom all creatures owe their love, honor, and respect, and this is made clear by the many proclamations for days of prayer, repentance and thanksgiving issued by the Continental Congress and by founding presidents.

The First Continental Congress was opened with an extended time of Bible reading and prayer, and prayer continued to be a vital part of their daily proceedings. During the Revolutionary War, no less than fifteen separate calls for days of prayer, repentance and thanksgiving were issued by the Continental Congress.

After being sworn in as president, George Washington issued a proclamation designating November 26, 1789 as a Day of Thanksgiving. The proclamation assumes the obligation of all citizens to acknowledge God's existence and to show honor to Him. It opened with the following statement.

> Whereas it is the duty of all Nations to acknowledge the providence of Almighty God, to obey his will, to be grateful for his benefits, and humbly to implore his protection and favor, and whereas both Houses of Congress have by their joint Committee requested me to recommend to the People of the United States a day of public thanksgiving and prayer to be observed by acknowledging with grateful hearts the many signal favors of Almighty God . . ..

The Declaration of Independence begins by acknowledging the Creator and recognizing that all human rights come from Him. This is the basis on which John Dickinson, chairman of the committee for the Declaration of Independence, declared in 1776,

> Our liberties do not come from charters for these are only the declarations of preexisting rights. They do not depend on parchment or seals; but come from the King of Kings and the Lord of all the earth.

Indeed, there was a consensus among the Founders that America had come forth by the Providential hand of God. Reflecting on the completed work of the Constitutional Convention, James Madison, the chief architect of the Constitution, saw God's handiwork in it all, and wrote,

> It is impossible for the man of pious reflection not to perceive in it a finger of that Almighty hand which has been so frequently and signally extended to our relief in critical stages of the Revolution.

Benjamin Rush was a physician from Philadelphia who signed the Declaration of Independence and led the state of Pennsylvania in ratifying the Constitution. He was even more blunt in his belief that the Almighty had influenced the formulation of the Constitution. He declared that he,

> As much believed the hand of God was employed in this work as that God had divided the Red Sea to give a passage to the children of Israel or had fulminated the Ten Commandments from Mount Sinai.

Indeed, although there was tolerance for those of various faiths, atheism was considered a detriment to good citizenship in early America. This was borne out in 1831 when a judge in the court of Chester County in the state of New York, threw out the testimony of a witness when the witness admitted he did not believe in the existence of God. The judge said that by his admission, the witness had, "destroyed all the confidence of the court in what he was about to say."

The judge said it was the first time he had met someone who did not acknowledge the existence of God. He also said that he knew of no case in a Christian country where a witness had been permitted to testify without such belief (Skousen, *The 5000 Year Leap*, 101).

It was the deep faith of America's founding generation that led to the adoption of "In God We Trust" as the nation's official motto and printed on all paper currency and coins. Although this motto was officially adopted in 1956, it had its beginnings in 1861 when Secretary of the Treasury, Salmon P. Chase, sent the following instructions to James Pollack, director of the mint at Philadelphia.

> Dear Sir: No nation can be strong except in the strength of God, or safe except in His defense. The trust of our people in God should be declared on our national coins. You will cause a device to be prepared without unnecessary delay with a motto expressing in the fewest and tersest words possible this national recognition.

This pervasive belief in God by America's Founders is reflected in the references to God and the verses of Scripture that abound on historical monuments in Washington D.C., Philadelphia and Boston. It is also reflected in the phrase "one nation under God" being part of the Pledge of Allegiance, a pledge that is repeated by every new citizen, and once was repeated every morning by school children across America.

No, America was not founded on secularism, Deism or atheism. America was founded on belief in the God of the Bible, the Creator, who in the words of Paul the Apostle, will "judge the world in righteousness" and hold each person accountable for their deeds. America's Founders agreed with William Penn, the founder of Pennsylvania, who said, "He who will not be governed by God must be ruled by tyrants."

Chapter 3

Pillar 2
Respect for the Bible as the Source of Ultimate Truth

When George Washington placed his hand on a Bible to take the oath of office it was no mere formality, but a declaration that the Bible would be the ultimate source of wisdom and guidance for his administration. He also once said, "It is impossible to rightly govern the world without God and the Bible" (Hyatt, *Pilgrims and Patriots*, 137).

While president, Washington's nephew, Robert Lewis, served as his secretary and lived with him. Lewis said that he had accidentally witnessed Washington's private devotions in his library both morning and evening and that on those occasions he had seen him in a kneeling posture with a Bible open before him, and that he believed such to have been his daily practice.

A ten-year project instituted to discover where the Founders got their ideas for America's founding documents found that by far the single most cited authority in their writings was the Bible. They were people of the Book and consciously and unconsciously used it as the standard for measuring all other writings both ancient and modern.

From the beginning, the Bible had been incorporated into all the learning of the schools in Colonial America. For example, *The New England Primer* coupled Bible verses and church doctrine with the learning of the ABCs. The letter "A," for example, was associated with "Adam" and the statement, "In Adam's fall, we sinned all." First graders in early America learned to read with their primer in one hand and their Bible in the other.

Knowing how the Founders esteemed and reverenced the Bible, it comes as no surprise that The First Continental Congress was opened with Bible reading and prayer. It is also no surprise that when Benjamin Franklin called the Constitutional Convention to Prayer, he quoted from both the Psalms and the Gospels (Hyatt, *Pilgrims and Patriots*, 143-44).

While he was at The College of New Jersey, now Princeton University, James Madison translated the Bible from Hebrew and Greek into English. Dr. D. James Kennedy and Jerry Newcombe were right when they said, "Madison's worldview was one shaped by the Bible more than any other source" (Hyatt, *Pilgrims and Patriots*, 146).

The Founders' respect for the Bible was highlighted when the first English Bible printed in America in 1782 included a recommendation from Congress. The producer of the Bible, Robert Aitken, had written a letter to Congress in which he asked for that government body's sanction on his work. In the letter, Aitken called this Bible, "a neat Edition of the Scriptures for the use in schools."

Congress enthusiastically responded to his request and offered the following recommendation to be included in this first English Bible printed in America.

> Resolved: That the United States in Congress assembled, highly approve the pious and laudable undertaking of Mr. Aitken, as subservient to the interest of religion as well as an instance of the progress of the arts in this country, and being satisfied from the above report, of his care and accuracy in the execution of the work they recommend this edition of the Bible to the inhabitants of the United States and hereby authorize him to publish this recommendation in the manner he shall think proper.

The Founders lived at a time when the European Enlightenment and its emphasis on reason was drawing many on the European continent away from the Bible. America's Founders, however, saw no dichotomy between the Bible and reason. The well-known Catholic scholar, William Novak, says,

> Everywhere that reason led, Americans found the Bible. If they read Francis Bacon, they found the Bible. If they read Isaac Newton or John Milton, they found the Bible. In Shakespeare, they found the Bible. In the world of the founders, the Bible was an unavoidable and useful rod of measurement, a stimulus to intellectual innovation.

This primary role of the Bible in America's founding was acknowledged by Andrew Jackson, America's 7th president, when he declared, "That book, sir, is the rock on which our Republic rests." It was also confirmed by the 26th president, Theodore Roosevelt, who said, "No other book of any kind ever written English has ever so affected the whole life of a people."

There is no question that the Bible played a primary role in the founding of America, supplying many of the ideas that the Founders incorporated into her founding documents. It is, therefore, almost inconceivable that the Bible is now banned from public schools and government officials are threatened with lawsuits for holding Bible studies with their colleagues.

This un-American hostility to the Bible is a marker showing how far the nation has fallen from its roots and serves as a wake-up call for Christians in America to pray for another great, national spiritual awakening.

Chapter 4

Pillar 3
Human Nature Has Been Flawed by Sin and Cannot be Trusted with Unlimited Power.

Marxism and modern liberalism claim that human nature is essentially good, and that people only need a revolutionary change of circumstances and institutions to improve and perfect their behavior. The Founders held no such utopian view of the human condition.

America's Founders held the traditional Christian belief that humanity had been created a noble creature in the image and likeness of God, but that this image had become marred because of the fall and sin (Genesis 1-3). Because the image was not erased, humanity is capable of very noble deeds; but since the image is marred, he is also capable of very dastardly deeds.

The historian, Benjamin Hart, wrote, "A central assumption of America's founders was original sin, meaning the corruption of man's character." "Take mankind in general," said Alexander Hamilton, "they are vicious." James Madison added, "If men were angels no government would be necessary,"

Although modern society does not want to hear about sin, human history cannot be understood apart from it. Only the Biblical account of the entry of sin into the world provides the context for understanding the wars, genocides, inquisitions, holocausts, and cruelties that have been an ongoing part of human history down to the present time.

Yes, salvation through Jesus Christ restores the image of God in mankind, but this restoration is a process that is not completed in this world. Humanity—even Christian humanity—in this flawed condition cannot be trusted with unlimited power.

Because of mankind's corrupt nature, a government is necessary to protect the good, punish the evil and maintain an ordered society. However, since corrupt human beings must administer any such government, they must have restraints placed on their exercise of civil power.

It was this mistrust of human nature that influenced the Founders to divide the powers of government into three branches and to provide checks and balances to keep any individual or group from gaining unlimited power. The Founders would agree with Sir John Acton who said, "Power corrupts; absolute power corrupts absolutely."

It is also why, in Section 9 of the Constitution, the Founders forbade the American government from granting honorific titles of nobility to anyone and forbade anyone holding a government office from accepting a title or office from a foreign king or state without the consent of Congress.

The Founders had a Biblical view of human nature and that is why they limited the powers of government and abolished aristocracy and hereditary privilege. Even then, said Washington, "We have probably had too good an opinion of human nature in forming our confederation."

Marxism and liberalism claim that the problem with human corruption stems from corrupt institutions. The Bible teaches, and America's Founders believed, the opposite. It is corrupt human beings who create corrupt institutions. The Founders, therefore, not only instituted a limited government, but also counted on Christianity to provide the moral and intellectual influence necessary for a stable society, for only a virtuous people could be a truly free people.

Chapter 5

Pillar 4
Christian Values are Essential for A Stable and Prosperous Nation.

In his Farewell address after serving two terms as America's first president, George Washington declared, "Of all the dispositions and habits which lead to political prosperity, religion [Christianity] and morality are *indispensable* supports." He goes on to say that the person who would "labor to subvert these great pillars of human happiness" can never claim to be an American patriot.

Thomas Jefferson was in complete agreement and he made Washington's Farewell Address required reading at the University of Virginia, which he had founded. Notice that Washington did not call religion optional. The word he used was "indispensable" and Jefferson obviously agreed. It should be remembered that when the Founders used the word "religion" they were referring to Christianity.

Jefferson may have had questions at times about certain aspects of Christian doctrine, but there is no question that he saw Christianity as providing the moral and intellectual system necessary for a stable society. Having read the Koran and the literature of ancient Greece, Rome, and the Enlightenment, he stated, "Of all the systems of morality that have come under my observations, none appear to me so pure as that of Jesus."

Jefferson's commitment to Christian values is why he closed all presidential documents with the appellation, "In the year of our Lord Christ." It is also why he took money from the federal treasury to pay for missionaries to work among the Kaskasia Indian tribe and to build them a building in which to worship.

Benjamin Franklin also expressed questions at times about certain aspects of Christian doctrine, but through his close friendship with George Whitefield, the most famous preacher of the Great Awakening, he became convinced that Christian values are necessary for a stable society. He once said, "The moral and religious system which Jesus Christ transmitted to us is the best the world has ever seen, or can see."

Franklin's commitment to Christian values for a stable society was borne out when the well-known Deist, Thomas Paine, sent him a manuscript copy of a book he had written challenging the idea of a providential God and other aspects of orthodox Christianity. Franklin refused to print the book, and in very strong language, he urged Paine not even to allow anyone else to see it. He wrote,

I would advise you, therefore . . . to burn this piece before it is seen by any other person; whereby you will save yourself a great deal of mortification by the enemies it may raise against you, and perhaps a good deal of regret and repentance. If men are so wicked with religion [Christianity], what would they be if without it (Hyatt, *Pilgrims and Patriots*, 142).

Benjamin Rush, who was a devout Christian, was also convinced that virtue and liberty walk hand in hand. He wrote,

The only foundation for a republic is to be laid in Religion [Christianity]. Without this there can be no liberty, and liberty is the object and life of all republican governments.

Yes, Washington, Jefferson, Franklin, Rush and all the Founders knew that the success of the nation they had formed hinged on the moral character of its citizens and their ability to govern themselves according to Christian values. This is why John Adams, in a 1798 address to the officers of the Massachusetts Militia, declared,

We have no government armed with power capable of contending with human passions unbridled by morality and religion . . . Our Constitution was made only for a moral and religious [Christian] people. It is wholly inadequate to the government of any other (Hyatt, *Pilgrims and Patriots*, 173).

Recent presidents have sought to export American style democracy to other nations apart from any connection to Christian virtue and morality. The Founders would say that such efforts are futile since true liberty cannot be had apart from the Gospel of Jesus Christ.

This dependence of liberty on Christian morality was expressed by John Adams two weeks before the adoption of the Declaration of Independence. In a letter to his cousin, Zabdiel, a minister of the Gospel, Adams wrote,

Statesmen, my dear sir, may plan and speculate for Liberty, but it is Religion [Christianity] and Morality alone, which can establish the Principles, upon which Freedom can securely stand (Hyatt, *Pilgrims and Patriots*, 174).

It was this emphasis on Christian morality tied with freedom that eventually brought about the end of slavery in America. Walter Williams, the brilliant black professor of economics at George Mason University, points out how slavery had been practiced by many civilizations throughout human history before it was brought to America. He then says that the unique thing about slavery in America was "the moral outrage against it."

This moral outrage was rooted in the Christian worldview that was promulgated throughout the land. Writing about the existence of slavery in his home state of Virginia in 1781, Jefferson expressed hope that it would soon be abolished and then warned,

> God who gave us life, gave us liberty. And can the liberties of a nation be thought secure when we have removed their only firm basis, a conviction in the minds of the people that these liberties are a gift from God? That they are not to be violated but with His wrath? Indeed, I tremble for my country when I reflect that God is just and that His justice cannot sleep forever (Hyatt, *Pilgrims and Patriots*, 160-61).

Many do not realize it, but Dr Martin Luther King Jr., in his "I Have a Dream" speech called for a return to the Christian vision of the Founders. He made it clear that he did not want America to dispense with her founding documents, but to live up to them. He declared his hope that one day,

This nation will rise up and live out the true meaning of its creed: "We hold these truths to be self-evident, that all men are created equal.

Showing that he understood these freedoms to be rooted in the country's Christian origins, Dr. King, who was a devout Christian, went on to say that he had a dream that one day all Americans—whether white or black—would be able to sing together the words of that Christian, patriotic hymn,

My country 'tis of Thee,
Sweet land of liberty, of Thee I sing.
Land where my fathers died,
Land of the Pilgrim's pride,
From every mountainside,
Let freedom ring!

The Founders did not believe that there could be liberty apart from virtue, or freedom apart from morality. Only Christianity offered the moral and intellectual underpinnings that would preserve the nation they had brought into existence. Novak is, therefore, correct in saying, "The founders did not believe the constitutional government they were erecting could survive without Hebrew-Christian faith."

Chapter 6

Pillar 5
Government Exists to Protect Faith and Freedom

No part of the Constitution has been so mangled and misapplied as that part of the First Amendment that reads, "Congress shall make no law concerning the establishment of religion or hindering the free exercise thereof." Secularists have wrenched this statement from its historical context and original intent and made it to mean, not freedom *of* religion, but freedom *from* religion.

In this new and novel approach to the First Amendment, atheists and agnostics are protected from being offended by anything religious. Based on this distortion, prayer and Bible reading have been banned from public schools, crosses and Ten Commandment displays have been removed from public buildings, and students have been told they cannot talk about their faith in God at graduation ceremonies.

The consequences have been disastrous. When this author was in high school in the early 1960s, the biggest problems were things like chewing gum in class, talking during class, being out of your seat without permission, and being late for class.

Now, after 50+ years of evicting everything Christian from the public schools, the problems now are school shootings, violence against teachers, teachers having sex with students, broken discipline and poor academics. This is what the Founders foresaw would happen if the pillars of Christian faith and morality were ever removed.

The First Amendment had noting to do with barring from the public square Christian teachings, which the Founders considered "indispensable" to the success of the nation. This was made clear when the day after voting to ratify the First Amendment, those same Founders issued a proclamation for a day of prayer and thanksgiving.

It was obvious to the founding generation that the First Amendment had nothing to do with secularizing America or banning faith in the public square. Congress continued to be opened with prayer and Bible reading and prayer continued to be a daily part of the normal school day in America. Presidents also continued to issue proclamations for special days of prayer and thanksgiving.

By implementing the First Amendment, the Founders were simply saying that America would never have a national, state church as had been the case in Europe since the time of Constantine. Indeed, it was from these oppressive state churches that their parents and grandparents had fled.

When Jefferson used the phrase "wall of separation" in a letter to a Baptist association, he was assuring them that the First Amendment guaranteed them protection from persecution by the state such as they had known in the Old World, and even in Jefferson's home state of Virginia. Jefferson saw the First Amendment as a unilateral wall erected to keep the government out of the church, not to keep the influence of the church out of government.

It is obvious to anyone who knows history that the First Amendment was not put in place to stifle Christianity or to be indifferent towards it. The words and actions of the Founders make this clear. This was also made clear by Joseph Story (1779-1845) who served as a Supreme Court justice for thirty-four years from 1811-1845. Commenting on the First Amendment, he said,

> We are not to attribute this prohibition of a national religious establishment to an indifference in religion, and especially to Christianity, which none could hold in more

reverence than the framers of the Constitution (Hyatt, *Pilgrims and Patriots*, 153).

That America's Founders relied on Christianity to maintain civil liberty was obvious to the young French sociologist, Alexis de Tocqueville, who came to America in 1831 to study her institutions. As a result of his research, he concluded that Americans had combined Christianity and civil liberty so intimately in their minds that it was impossible to make them conceive of one without the other.

According to Tocqueville, this linking of faith with civil liberty was the reason for their passion to spread the Gospel to the American frontier where new settlements were springing up. He wrote,

> I have known of societies formed by the Americans to send out ministers of the Gospel in the new Western states, to found schools and churches there, lest religion should be suffered to die away in those remote settlements, and the rising states be less fitted to enjoy free institutions than the people from whom they came. I met with New Englanders who abandoned the country in which they were born in order to lay the foundations of Christianity and of freedom on the banks of the Missouri, or in the prairies of Illinois.

Thus, religious zeal is warmed in the United States by the fires of patriotism.

From his observations, Tocqueville concluded, "From the beginning, politics and religion contracted an alliance which has never been dissolved" (Hyatt, *Pilgrims and Patriots*, 168).

The Founders would be astonished to see how the First Amendment has been distorted by modern secularists into a weapon against religious liberty, the very thing they meant to protect. Their simple purpose was to make sure that Christianity would be protected from government intrusion and that no denomination would ever be singled out for special favors by the government.

Chapter 7

Recovering Faith & Freedom in America

Yes, America was founded as a Christian nation. This is not to be equated with a theocracy where individuals claim a direct mandate from God to rule and govern a people. The Founders had rejected that sort of thinking, but they had not rejected Christianity itself, for they considered Christianity to be necessary for the nation's success and survival.

We have already seen the Founders commitment to Christian principles and values. It comes, therefore, as no surprise that John Adams, nearly four decades after the American Revolution, would declare,

> The general principles on which the fathers achieved independence were . . . the general principles of Christianity. Now I will avow that I then believed, and now believe, that those general principles of Christianity are as eternal and immutable as the existence and attributes of God (Hyatt, *Pilgrims and Patriots*, 163-64).

America as a Christian nation was understood as late as 1892 as expressed in the Supreme Court ruling of "Church of the Holy Trinity *vs* The United States."

After reviewing thousands of historical documents, the nation's highest Court declared,

> Our laws and our institutions must necessarily be based upon and embody the teachings of The Redeemer of mankind. It is impossible that it should be otherwise; and in this sense and to this extent our civilization and our institutions are emphatically Christian . . . From the discovery of this continent to the present hour, there is a single voice making this affirmation . . . we find everywhere a clear recognition of the same truth that this is a Christian nation (Hyatt, *Pilgrims and Patriots*, 167)

The pillars of the American Republic were obviously still in place at the time of this ruling. Today, however, it is obvious that those pillars are eroded and seriously damaged. Years of relentless attacks on Christianity by secularists and neglect by the church have taken their toll. Many believe they are damaged beyond repair and that the American Republic our Founders brought into existence is forever gone.

I am not so pessimistic. At critical times during our nation's history God has intervened with national awakenings that have restored virtue to the populace and saved the nation from utter ruin. These include the Second Great Awakening (1800-1830), the Great

Prayer Awakening of 1857-58, and other local, regional, and national revivals throughout her history.

These were not man-made religious events, but Divine visitations from heaven that transformed American culture. That is what we must have today. Not a hyped religious event by a skilled crowd manipulator, but a true outpouring of the Holy Spirit as promised in Acts 2:17, and as happened in the First Great Awakening that brought this nation into existence.

In 2010 this writer experienced a Divine visitation that restored his hope that America could see another such spiritual awakening that would stem the tide of secularism and restore virtue and sanity to our land. This, however, will not come from Washington D.C., but from those who name the name of the Lord. The promise of II Chronicles 7:14 is still valid. *If My people who are called by My name will humble themselves and pray . . . I will hear from heaven and heal their land.*

America's pillars can be restored, but it will require a purposeful and prayerful commitment by a dedicated few to the following vision: (1) We must educate about America's Christian origins; (2) We must stand strong in Biblical and historical truth; and (3) We must pray for another Great Awakening across the land.

If you will join me in this vision, I would love to hear from you.

Selected Bibliography

Amos, Gary and Richard Gardiner. *Never Before in History: America's Inspired Birth*. Richardson, TX: Foundation for Thought and Ethics, 1998.

Barton, David. *The Role of Pastors & Christians in Civil Government*. Aledo, TX: Wallbuilder Press, 2003.

Federer, William J. *America's God and Country Encyclopedia of Quotations*. St. Louis: Amerisearch, 2013.

Franklin, Benjamin. *The Autobiography of Benjamin Franklin*. New York: Airmont, 1965.

Hall, Verna M., Ed. *The Christian History of the American Revolution*. San Francisco: The Foundation for Christian Education, 1976.

Hart, Benjamin. *Faith & Freedom: The Christian Roots of American Liberty.* Dallas: Lewis and Stanley, 1988.

Hyatt. Eddie L. *Pilgrims and Patriots*. Grapevine. TX: Hyatt Press, 2016.

Skousen, Cleon W. *The 5000 Year Leap*. USA: Nat'l Center for Constitutional Studies, 2006.

Kennedy, D. James and Jerry Newcombe. *What If America Were a Christian Nation Again?* Nashville: Thomas Nelson, 2003.

Marshall, Peter and David Manuel. *The Light and the Glory*. Grand Rapids: Fleming H. Revell, 1977.

Novak, William. *On Two Wings: Humble Faith and Common Sense at the American Founding*. San Francisco: Encounter Books, 2002.

About the Author

Dr. Eddie L. Hyatt is a seasoned minister of the Gospel with over 45 years of ministerial experience as a pastor, Bible teacher and Professor of Theology. He holds the Doctor of Ministry from Regent University as well as the Master of Divinity and a Master of Arts from Oral Roberts University. He has authored several books, including *2000 Years of Charismatic Christianity*, which is used as a textbook in colleges and seminaries around the world. Eddie's current passion is to call America back to its founding principles of freedom and Spiritual awakening. He is doing this through his writings and by conducting "America Reawakening" events in which he shows how America was birthed out of a Great Awakening and then calling on his audience to commit to pray for another national, spiritual awakening. He resides in Grapevine, TX with his wife, Dr. Susan Hyatt, where they are establishing the Int'l Christian Women's Hall of Fame and Ministry Center (https://www.gwtwchristianwomenshalloffame.com). If you would like to make contact with him, his email address is dreddiehyatt@gmail.com. His website address is www.eddiehyatt.com.

For discounts on bulk orders
of this book, send an email to
dreddiehyatt@gmail.com.

Other Books by Drs. Eddie & Susan Hyatt

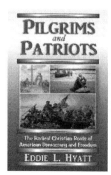
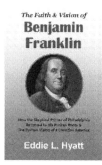
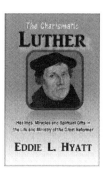

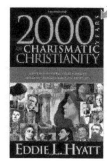
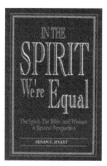
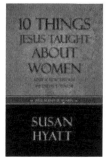

These and other materials are
available from Amazon and from
www.eddiehyatt.com and
www.godswordtowomen.org.

Made in the USA
Columbia, SC
06 December 2021